Behind The Hijab

Rabina Khan

Contributing Writers:

I0109014

Nargis Rahman
Zahrah Awaleh
Bubli Miah
Iram Riza Syed
Andersen
Sarah Butler
Shakti Maya
Central Foundation Girls' School
Hamida Yasmin
Penny Wrout
Shahida Rahman
Ruzina Ahad
Ayesha Mazumder
Preetha Leela Chockalingam

Foreword:

The Hon Baroness Pola Uddin

i

Copyright ©Monsoon Press

All rights reserved. No part of this publication may be reproduced, stored in a retrieval system or transmitted in any form or by any means, electronic, mechanical, audio, visual or otherwise, without prior written permission of the copyright owner. Nor can it be circulated in any form of binding or cover other than that in which it is published and without similar conditions including this condition being imposed on the subsequent purchaser.

ISBN 978-0-9557267-1-2

Cover Design by Duncan Bamford
http://www.insightillustration.co.uk

Edited by Rabina Khan
http://www.rabinakhan.com

&

Jan Andersen
http://www.creativecopywriter.org

Published by
Monsoon Press in collaboration with Perfect Publishers

MONSOON PRESS
Oxford House Arts Centre
Derbyshire St
London E2 5HG
http://www.monsoon press.org

PERFECT PUBLISHERS
http://www.perfectpublishers.co.uk

Acknowledgements

I wish to express my deepest gratitude to all the writers for their wonderful contributions, not to mention the immense time, effort and commitment they gave, which made the publication of this book possible.

Thank you for taking time out from your busy schedules to agree to meet me in various cafés and fast food venues around London, which I am certain has helped to keep the catering industry in business!

Monsoon Press would also like to acknowledge the support of the Arts Council in the publication of Behind the Hijab and in particular our Grants Officer, Charles Beckett.

Rabina Khan, Monsoon Press

Introduction

The Hijab is a controversial subject that has sparked various debates from politicians, community leaders, writers and media figures. In 2006, following a meeting with a woman wearing a face veil, Jack Straw expressed his concerns about women wearing the full veil, saying that that he felt uncomfortable about talking to someone 'face-to-face' who he could not see. Although he did say that he absolutely defended the right of any woman to wear a headscarf and that wearing the full veil broke no laws, he still felt that the conversation would be of greater value if the lady took the covering from her face.

At the time I was working in a school where a number of young Muslim girls raised their concerns as to why there was so much attention on the Hijab. They could not understand why a nun could cover her head and be respected, yet a Muslim woman would cover her head and be called oppressed. What is the difference?

The true underlying principle of the Hijab is modesty. Modesty is a virtue expected within Islam, for through it a person librates themselves from egotism and falsehoods and embraces a vision of life that encompasses humility. Islam has often been criticised that its texts need to be reformed. It is actually not the text that needs to be reformed, but our interpretations of the text. It is only when we understand the text that can we extract the objectives and thus use the means.

There are no specific Islamic laws relating to the attire of Muslim women, but there are directions as to what is morally, socially, spiritually and rationally preferable and permissible. Thus, Muslims are required to use their common sense and adapt Islamic Laws and adjust accordingly. The claim that wearing the Hijab is obligatory, is simply not true; it's a question of personal choice, in the same way that young Westerners choose to wear baseball caps or "hoodies," or elderly women choose to wear headscarves.

However, it is not just about the right to wear the Hijab or not, but the personal journey that the heart of a Muslim woman makes to reach the decision of whether or not she wishes to wear the Hijab.

Fundamental human rights such as the freedom of speech, expression, religion, belief and education have been challenged in recent years, not least since the wave of heinous terrorist attacks around the world. Many people in Western Society have come to view Hijab wearing women with suspicion and even contempt, assuming that since they are openly identifying themselves as Muslims, they must, therefore, have some hidden agenda or sinister motive.

This book provides a personal insight into the way in which one's personal clothing choice has impacted the lives of Muslim women living in Britain, in addition to unbiased views from non-Muslim writers. The contributors' feelings are expressed though heartfelt poetry and candid, thought-provoking editorials.

Foreword

by The Hon Baroness Uddin

I am delighted to have been asked to contribute a Foreword for this book, which addresses head on some of the issues surrounding women who wear the hijab. It addresses often misunderstood issue of ethnic dress code in a Western multi cultural, multi faith society.

Having been born in Bangladesh, raised and residing in London, I am an internationalist in the clothes that I wear, although I am all too aware of the many blinkered commentators who freely express their opinion of women of the East End, where a third of the population is Bangladeshi, as though clothes define their intellect and characters. Neither my grandmothers nor my mother wore the veil. I do not, except when praying or visiting places of worships and elderly relatives.

When asked of my view, I say that the hijab is an adapted 21st century code of dressing for many women in the developed nation, without necessarily having any references to their cultural heritage and upbringing. Also, that as a British citizen who values individual freedom, I am absolutely certain in my advocacy for the right for women to choose how and what they wish to wear. Importantly, in a country with such proud history of cultural, social and religious diversity, we have to support choices that women make in the way they wish to live, whatever religion they choose to embrace, or however they wish to practice it. I do think we should pay less attention to what is adorning people's head and instead look at the institutional barriers that preclude them from jobs and equal access to public life.

Hopefully, this book will serve to enlighten many that have preconceived ideas about women who wear the hijab and perhaps even allow an insight into a greater level of understanding and mutual respect. This book expresses the obvious and that is that beneath the veil are intelligent, articulate, humorous, ambitious and fun loving individuals; real women making a significant contribution to British society, not oppressed clones, just as simple and or extraordinary as all other women in our communities. I am confident that in not such distant futures, we will see greater reflection of such women in drama and theatre productions and other spheres of our cultural reflections and civic life.

This book is beautifully balanced by views of non-Muslim women and shows that irrespective of ethnicity or religion, we are all in fact subjected to, and influenced by a specific set of dress codes depending upon both the social and our own cultural context. We have come to accept all too readily, as one of our civilising norms, that women should openly reveal their bodies in the name of freedom and gender equity. If this is true, then I believe we are all now grown up enough to accept that many women in our country also can and must be allowed to choose

Contents

Thoughts of a Muslim

I look around and wonder...
What is the meaning of my observations in the world?
What is the meaning of the things happening around me?
What is the meaning of my very existence?
I look around and wonder...
Subhallah! The moon, the sun, the stars;
How beautifully they have been created
And how beautifully they are going about their business.
I stop and wonder...
How can I deny the existence of a Creator?
How can there be creations without a Creator?
How can the creations emerge from nowhere?
Don't you think there must be a reason why we are living in this world?
Don't you think there is a reason why the Prophet (SAW) and the
Prophets before him came into this world?
Don't you think there is a reason why all the historical events that happened in this
beautiful religion happened for a reason?
Islam is a dip in the ocean.
The more you learn, the more your heart will quench to seek more.
If you believed this world to be a temporary abode,
A test to gain the comfort and pleasure in the next life,
Wouldn't you change your behaviour?
Wouldn't you change your thinking and your ways?
I am no scientist, nor a philosopher, but a simple Muslim
And these are the thoughts of a Muslim.

©Nargis Rahman

The Muslim Woman

See how she walks swiftly and gently,
With her modesty shining through.
See how her eyes never rise,
Even at the sight of temptation.
See how her confidence carries her through
The sniggering groups of people.
See how strong willed she is,
With no fear whatsoever.
See how respected she is,
With her outstanding character.
Have you ever stopped to think
Why she is like this?
Have you ever thought,
"What drives her to be different amongst other women?"
Have you ever thought,
"What makes her so special to the people of
understanding?"
She is a pious Muslim Woman
Who far exceeds the value of the treasures of this world.

©Nargis Rahman

When You Look At Me

When you look at me,
What do you see?
Someone restricted within her beliefs?
Cannot think or gain freedom like everyone else?
When you look at me,
What do you see?
Someone illiterate, backward and boring?
Well, I beg to differ;
This is not me.
The true me holds my belief with dignity,
The true me respects myself,
Enough not to expose it to the pleasures of the world.
You see, I know my worth is much more than the worldly
temptations.
The true me doesn't have to boast about the knowledge I
hold
In order to use it.
To the world I may be boring and backwards,
But to me I am fulfilling my Islamic duties.

©Nargis Rahman

The Simple Garment

I am a Muslim,
A proud Muslim,
A lady with strong beliefs.
Why should I hide that fact?
The comments, the looks, the sniggering;
Don't care what people think,
I will still hold my head high,
I will still walk with bliss and dignity.
So simple is the garment,
Yet so effective at its job,
Protecting me from the eyes of the world,
Reminding me of Allah.
Stop....look...and think,
Do you truly want to be amongst the ignorant?
Do you truly want the lustful world?
Is it really worth sacrificing your Imaan?

©Nargis Rahman

4

Who Am I?

I am a flower with no smell,
Yet happily swaying in the breeze.
I am a flower firm in the pot,
As I have accepted what Allah has pre-ordained for me.
Taking the advice of my mentor,
I am content with the decision I have made.
With no complaints, nor hard feelings, I fear Allah (the
Mighty) alone,
And put all trust in Him.
Do you not see the world does not matter to me,
As I have left it behind.
Only in love with spirituality I await to be placed in my
eternal abode,
Which Allah has promised His servants.
I do not expect the world to understand who I am,
But if Allah is happy with me, that is most sufficient to me.
What does this tell you about me?

©Nargis Rahman
30 December 2004

Aishah, One of the Wives of the Prophet (SAW)

Peace be upon you Lady Aishah (RA),
The daughter of Abu Bakr Siddique (RA).
I honour and respect you Oh Aishah for showing to the world
that a woman can be a teacher of Scholars and experts.
Your life is such an encouragement to us all,
As you have shown that a woman can influence and inspire men and women alike.
Oh Aishah (RA), your words are studied in faculties of literature
And your legal sayings are studied in colleges of Law.
But yet, you have shown that a woman can also fulfil her duties as a wife and a daughter.
Oh Allah, please help us all to learn from this great lady –
Ameen.

©Nargis Rahman
30 December 2004

Footnote

Dedicated to the honourable lady Aishah (RA) who was one of the mothers of the Believers and one of the 4 best women in Islam.
On her own authority, she narrated over 2000 hadeeth and because of her strength in personality she was a leader in every field in knowledge and in society.
Subhallah! What a great woman!

About the Author:

Nargis Rahman is a Business Studies' graduate from Sheffield Hallam University and is currently working in the Department for Work and Pensions (DWP) in Communications in Sheffield. She does a lot of community work and engages herself in Dawah activities, such as appearing on Noor TV to talk about Islamic subjects. Nargis has also been on Channel S on community news. She has recently been invited by Sheffield Hallam University to give an inspiring talk about her journey in Islam during their Islamic Awareness week.

Nargis is an Islamic poet and her work has been highlighted on Noor TV and in various publications, newspapers and websites. She is classed as a role model to the young and the old.

Hijabi – A Monologue

©Zahrah Awaleh

When people look at me I wonder who they see. Do they see a young Muslim woman and think, "Poor thing, it must be hot in that. Her husband must make her wear it." Perhaps they think that I'm another refugee that's come to the UK on "false pretences" just so that I can have a better life, compliments of the welfare system. Or do they live in mortal fear that I may have a grudge against Britain, because it allowed its government to invade and ruin Iraq, so much so that I'm willing to kill myself and many other people in an act of revenge?

A lot of people may think that I'm all of those I've mentioned: suppressed wife, refugee (i.e. social parasite) and potential terrorist. So what can I do about it?

Whenever I open my mouth and talk in public, a few people will always gape at me as though they've seen an exotic anomaly because of my perfect English accent. They must have expected one that's more tinged with my mother tongue, so when they listen more closely and realise that English *is* my mother tongue, you can almost see their brains flip-flopping through the surprised expressions on their faces. If I'm in a good mood, then I find moments like this amusing. When I'm not in a good mood, then it's just plain annoying and I feel like growling at them.

I tend to just get on with what I'm doing, which isn't that much different from what most other people are doing; getting on a bus or train to work or shopping, taking my kids to school, or going to the gym. Yes, Muslim women *do* go to the gym and they even go the hairdressers too! You may laugh, but we do like to take care of ourselves when we get the time. The hijab isn't a barrier to that, but you may think, "What's the point of going to the hairdressers? Who's going to see it anyway?" Well, if that

8

was the case, then hijabis (i.e. those who wear hijab) would just let themselves go. However, hijabis do want to look good, just not in the same way that fashion dictates. Some of us like to follow the trends of the season, so much so that we look a bit confused. I've seen several hijabi teenagers sporting well-made-up faces and wearing tight tops with pedal pushers, fish net stockings and high heels!? However, the older hijabis are a tad more conservative and have the most boring hemlines in the world that don't reveal their legs, no matter what.

The hijab just isn't an issue for me; I just try to be genuine with people, but I don't fall into a typical Muslim stereotype. Some men get a bit flustered when they meet me and don't know whether to shake my hand or give me direct eye contact. Well, at least they're aware of some of the issues around Muslim mannerisms! A word of advice; if you're not sure, keep your hands by your sides and see if *she* greets you first with a handshake. As for eye contact, you'll be surprised how most Muslim women can handle it perfectly well, so long as it's got natural pauses, otherwise you may look like a stalker!

My hijab has always been my choice, not something my parents, relatives, husband or even friends pushed me into. It's part of my identity and a sign of my faith in God. Around the time that I put it on, I was a teenager doing all sorts of crazy chemical things to my hair. After I put on the hijab, it was quite a relief to allow my hair to be natural and not worry about its *swing rate* and smoothness. It was quite a political statement for me to do this and plait it, rather than give in to the adverts for black women's hair products and aspire to a more "modern" look. This is what a lot of black women aspire to because it's what's deemed by society to be an acceptable image of beauty; it's white, shiny and cultured. I don't really care if black women want to burn their hair into line. The point is to have the *choice* to go natural or use chemical relaxers and *not judge* anyone

9

or be judged for choosing one way or the other. Personally, I just don't want to be a slave to my hair or any other part of my body. I just want to get dressed and get on with my day. I don't wear make-up, nor do I regularly scrutinise my grey hairs and colour them over. I'm just not interested. I suppose I sound a bit like a man. I like what India Arie has to say about the topic in her song, "I Am Not My Hair":

> Good hair means curls and waves
> Bad hair means you look like a slave
> At the turn of the century
> It's time for us to redefine who we be
> You be shaving it off like a South African beauty
> Get it on lock like Bob Marley
> You can rock it straight like Oprah Winfrey
> If it's not what's on your head, it's what's underneath
> and say, hey
>
> I am not my hair, I am not this skin
> I am not your expectation, no
> I am not my hair, I am not this skin
> I am a soul that lives within.

As for the terminology, let's get the difference straight between hijab and niqab. The hijab goes by various other names, such as the veil or headscarf. As a side point, I'd like to highlight the fact that the term 'hijabi' is a lovely fusion of Arabic and English: British hijabis who wear the hijab have taken the Arabic noun 'hijab' and added on the English suffix 'i' to make a hybrid adjective that's truly and uniquely British.

The hijab is normally worn so it covers the head, neck, shoulders and chest, but can have other interpretations. All Muslim scholars agreed that it's obligatory for Muslim women to wear it, although they cite exceptions to the rule as well e.g. if it's an obstacle to accessing education or employment, as it is in some countries where it's banned. As for the niqab, it's also known as the face veil, full veil, or just veil. I can see why people get confused, so I call it niqab or face veil in English. This covers the face either leaving it partially or completely covered. According to the majority of Muslim scholars, this type is not obligatory, but a minority of women wear it perhaps because they believe it makes them more devout, culturally acceptable or helps them to fit into a Muslim community where it's the norm, e.g. somewhere like Oldham or Burnley, or even Tower Hamlets in East London.

Over the years there has been much controversy over Muslim women's dress that has caught the attention of the British press; the jilbab (long dress) story where Shabina Begum won her appeal for her right to wear it in school; Aishah Azmi who lost her case at her employment tribunal in October 2006 and following that was sacked from her school because of her refusal to take off her face veil in the classroom with a male teacher there; and then, of course, there was the issue of Jack Straw asking one of his Muslim female constituents to take off her face veil during one of his surgeries (after spending 30 years representing the majority Muslim community in Blackburn and not saying a peep about the face veil?!)

In my view, modest clothing comes in many forms that incorporate the local culture and fashions as well as the current social context. No one lives in a vacuum, so no singular type of dress for Muslim women can be assumed to be monolithic; every generation has to work towards creating dress styles that work for them according to their time, place and usage. You could say it's a continuous experiment to put Islamic notions of modest dress for women into action; that's the challenge. It would be extremely boring if all Muslim women worldwide wore the same dress; we'd all look like clones. No one has the right to say one style is better than another; that judgment should be left to God.

I'm tired of the debate over the "proper dress code" of Muslim women. Muslim women are human beings and first and foremost people need to get along with each other and learn about one another. In this post-9/11 era in which we're living, people are naturally wary of Muslims; men and women. I think Muslims shouldn't be apologetic, but we need to think deeply not just about our "awrah," but our about our aura as well. "Awrah" is an Islamic term used to describe the parts of the body that require modest covering due to their ability to cause sexual arousal i.e. between the naval and the knees for men and everything but the face, hands and feet for women. As a practising Muslim, I think we spend too much time on worrying about if we're getting our awrah right when we've actually got that one covered.

What a lot of us are really missing and are so obviously lacking is good aura; the ability to connect with people on a positive and genuine level without fear or prejudice. This is not just a fault that Muslims possess, since most people have lost the ability to even connect with themselves and their families, this being due to the increasingly consumerist society that we live in and the faster pace of life in general. The traditional Sufi paths have always taught the importance of self awareness, good conduct and good aura towards all of creation. The self-help movement is currently trying to remedy this massive problem too and a growing number of Muslims are joining it as well in order to remedy a plethora of social problems within and without Muslim communities.

When it comes to the dress of hijabis in Britain today, it comes in all sorts of different shapes and sizes. For example, all-in-black like in Saudi, to pin stripped suit, to urban smart-casual. That's all good. However, what's equally as important is that Muslims practise self-awareness, good conduct and good aura in every sphere of their lives and put aside their preferred interpretation of Islam for the one that promotes the common good for *all* of society.

About the Author:

Zahrah Awaleh was born in Scunthorpe, South Humberside in 1974, now located in North Lincolnshire, England. The town was a booming steel town when her father arrived and settled there in the 1950s. Consequently, her mother joined him there with the two eldest children in 1972.

Shortly after her father's death in 1984, the family moved to Sheffield, South Yorkshire, where Zahrah completed her secondary education in 1990. In the same year, the family moved to London where she later read Arabic at the School of Oriental and African Studies (SOAS). She returned there to read a Masters in Islamic Studies after working in Hargeisa, Somaliland with the United Nations Population Fund (UNFPA).

It was through the UNFPA and other UN agencies and NGOs in Hargeisa that Zahrah was exposed to campaigns against Female Genital Mutilation (FGM). This experience had a profound effect and lead to the writing of her Masters dissertation, which was based on the thesis that FGM is antithetical to Islam. Following her Masters, Zahrah went on to work with the London-based NGO Foundation for Women's Health, Research & Development (FORWARD), which runs national and international projects and campaigns against FGM and other forms of gender violence.

Zahrah holds a Post Graduate Diploma and Qualification in Careers Guidance and currently works as a Careers Adviser with Connexions in London. She has also contributed to Silent Voices, published in 2007 by Monsoon Press.

Zahrah is married with two children and lives in Ilford, Essex. If you would like to contact her via e-mail, her address is: z_awaleh@yahoo.com

The Death of Me

©Bubli Miah

I recently died. But the death of the "Me" who once was, wasn't celebrated by anyone but me. Funny innit?

I have been a fully fledged "hijabi" for the best part of a week or two now and after much silent observation of my family, my "friends" and of people around me, I think I now know why no one celebrated the death of Moloko and the re-birth of Me.

The uneducated, the narrow-minded and thick-headed members of our society pigeonhole people who wear a hijab. The fears they have are all pretty obvious. You get the cracks about the Taliban, you get the looks that tell you "you scare me, 'cause you're a fundamentalist," and you get the whispers that suggest people think you're a crazy bombing, Allah-preaching, bloody idiot who probably has really bad hair.

The 'friends' in my life laugh and say, "Don't worry, it's a phase. You know what she's like; she will be back to normal soon." They feel this way because they haven't taken the time to ask me, "Hey, what's up with that?" and wait for an answer. And I guess they never will, because it's different and different is sometimes scary. I get it.

I could sit here and justify why society is wrong and my "friends" are dickheads, but I can't be bothered and I have no desire to. If this is what you think and/or if you can't be bothered to take the time to find out what's going on with me, then fine. I really don't care.

My decision to wear a hijab didn't come from a sudden realization that this is what I should be doing. Nor did it come from an incessant moaning from my Mother who made me do it. Nor did it come from being brainwashed by some Fundu's who want me to join their gang and wish jihad on the infidels. It came about one cold day when I

15

couldn't find a hat to match my outfit and the desire to keep my head warm, and from a long few months of soul searching and wanting, almost needing some sense of direction, some comfort, something to change in my life to make it more meaningful; to not feel so lost, to not feel so desperate. I needed something to make me happy and justify my existence.

And I found it. It's called Islam.

OK, so wrapping my head up might not seem like a life changing experience to you, but you know what, it doesn't have to. It's actually not the head wrapping that is significant, which is what makes me laugh about the reactions I have been getting. It's how embracing my faith and my religion makes me feel. And if something as simple as a hijab and a few prayers makes me happy, why is it wrong, or bad, or weird? It may be all these things to you because it's not part of who you think I am, because you think I have no depth. It's not the Moloko you know... [correction; the Moloko you think you know].

Sometimes in life we do things we would never have imagined we would and it's those things that better our lives and make us feel happy. If you don't feel happy every day of your life, if you don't feel like you have a path, or a reason, then why are you here? It's a pretty pathetic existence wouldn't you say? I would, because it's how I had been feeling for so long, it was driving me to despair!

Now? Now I feel at peace. At peace with the world being messed up, at peace with my family being the way they are and at peace with where my life has taken me and will take me. I am at peace and I am happy.

However much you think wearing a hijab is restrictive and makes women docile or stupid or less deserving of respect from people, or that we can't be "fun" or go out anymore, then again, you're wrong. It's the complete opposite. It's liberating. It's powerful.

16

I walk with my head held high, higher than I did when I didn't sport a hijab. And even though it sometimes makes my ears itch and makes me hot, I don't hate it.

Self respect I have. Nice hair I have. Now I also have purpose and a reason and it feel fabulous.

Marcel Proust once said time changes people, but it doesn't alter the image people retain of them.

You can remember me the way you want to, but I am here and I'm not the same. And if you don't like it? I don't give a shit.

"People believe I am what they see Me as, rather than what they do not see. But I am the Great Unseen, not what I cause Myself to be in any particular moment. In a sense, I am what I am not. It is from the Am-notness that I come, and to it I always return."

I wish I could take the credit for making something so profound up, but I can't. It is a quote from American author, Neale Donald Walsch, but it sums up the point of this note.

Since my new head 'accessory' and since my last hijab entry, I have been asked a lot of weird things and received a lot of strange reactions. Today, for instance, some of the guys at work questioned me about Islam and were stunned that I didn't know the answers to what were probably simple questions. They were almost shocked that I didn't shout 'jihad jihad' when they insulted my religion; and the fact that I choose to instead question them back about their non-belief.

I find the perceptions people have of me, whether they know me or not, have become somewhat distorted. Take these Muppets at work for example. One is dating a Pakistani Muslim and the other has a Muslim convert sister/brother in law. They also know me from my wild child days. So just because I'm sporting a hijab, they assume that I must know why the Quran says this and why the Prophet said that. Why? Does putting a scarf on mean I become all knowledgeable all of a sudden? Well does it? I kind of wish it did, but it doesn't.

I'm learning things everyday from my Urban Family, but it's a slow process. Take the strangers that I pass on the street as another example. The other day, a lady across the road watched me as she walked ALL the way down the road, still watching me over her shoulder as she got further away. All I was doing was sitting at the bus stop. I wasn't even picking my nose. I don't know if she was waiting for me to pull a bomb out of my arse and kill myself or run around in a circle saying, "I'm a solider of Allah!" Either way, I'm sure she wanted to be one of those "innocent bystanders" you see on the BBC who say, "Yes and I just KNEW something was going to happen. I could feel it. I could see it in her eyes. I am traumatised."

Next, take the people I know. They suddenly think I spend all day listening to Nasheeds and reading the Quran. However "good" that might be for my soul, I'm not doing that!! I still like Sex and the City, I still smoke, I still use swear words and I still call everyone "Butters!"

Take the stupid boys on Facebook. They see my picture and think ,"Rah, nice simple looking chick… let me throw her a line and reel her in 'cause she won't cuss me; she looks to sweet and she's probably never lipsed a boy in her life" WRONG! (Hate to admit it but I've lipsed plenty in my heyday. Uffers. Instead of reeling me in, they reel backwards in shock when I bury them with my smart arse comments, making them feel stupid.

Leonardo da Vinci once said that all our knowledge has its origins in our perceptions. I once said perceptions are not always right.

> I am what I am.
> I am what you see.
> I am what you do not see.

At any given moment, I just am.

Judge me by what's in my head, not by what's on it

Yesterday, one of the boys at work made a passing comment about forgetting what I looked like without a hijab. Amused, I told him unless he proposed and became my husband, my luscious locks for him would stay a distant memory.

This boy, whom I quite like then said something that shocked and confused me. It went something like this: "If you don't take that thing off your head tomorrow, I will never talk to you again."Slightly shocked and dumbfounded, I did the only thing I could think of at the time. Laughed it off. As I made my way home, dodging speeding cars and sleazy London Lite distributors, the more I thought about it, the more angry I became. Why did he say that? What did he mean? Was he serious? Why did my hijab bother him? Did it make him uncomfortable? Why did it make him uncomfortable? What was his problem?

When I got in to work today, he said, "Ah man, you so didn't listen to me. What's up with that?!" I showed him my middle finger and carried on drinking my latte and checking Facebook and my 18 notifications.

I suddenly stopped and thought, "Hang on, WHO the hell does he think he is? How DARE he objectify me, insult me, my beliefs, my religion, my choice. How DARE he give me an ultimatum as to whom I choose to be and what I choose to do? What the hell is that about?

Enraged, I emailed his boss and his boss's boss:

"Yesterday XXX made a comment and I wasn't too sure whether he was joking or being serious...but regardless of whether he was or not.... I was quite shocked and offended by what he said. I'm confused because, if anyone should understand my Islamic beliefs, it would be

him (being a Muslim and all), but yet, he discriminated against me because I choose to wear a hijab?? Yesterday, he actually said 'If you wear that tomorrow, I won't talk to you again.' And this morning, he said, "Cha, what happened, you didn't listen to me.' Does that mean he won't talk to me until I take it off ??? Or that I can expect a series of similar comments during my time here? I mean, it takes a lot to offend me, but I think this is crossing the line. I shouldn't feel uncomfortable coming into work, or intimidated for my choice of religion and/or clothing. I just thought I would let you know. Bubli"

They replied:

"I've spoken to XXX at length regards to this. He is adamant he neither intended to offend or discriminate against you or your beliefs, which incidentally I do believe. I personally think he was perhaps being an idiot rather than offensive. He's feels he has a strong enough working relationship with you to have a joke – which with hindsight may have "crossed the line" I have spoken to him about the importance of respecting other people's beliefs and choices - I am confident this won't happen again. If you feel uncomfortable regards to this issue in the future then feel free to discuss this with either of us."

Shirley Chisholm once said, "In the end, anti-black, anti-female and all forms of discrimination are equivalent to the same thing – anti-humanism".

Do not de-humanise me. I am more than a hijab.

About the Author:

I am a 25-year-old Events Manager working in the City of London and living as a Bacheloress in North London. Some describe me as a riddle wrapped up in an enigma, others say I have an identity crisis. I say I'm a British Bengali who grew up struggling with the idea of Bengali-ness vs. English-ness like many of my peers. My dream career in Events Management funds my ridiculous obsession with shoes and world travel. I like to read, to dance and to paint.

I enjoy writing about real subjects that give the world a true insight into my community and what we struggle with as Muslims, as Women, as Brits and as Bengalis – all rolled into one. My inspiration comes from growing up in a highly dysfunctional family, a community that spurned me for being different, friends that never understood me and a lifetime of questions I still have that no one seems to have answers to.

My writing can be classed as the life and times of a British Bengali living in London and how 20-something single Asian women cope with the day to day pressures of who we are, how we move between pseudo personalities/communities, as well as how it makes us the people we are that stand before you.

Image Matters

©Iram Riza Syed

Several days after 7/7, I was on the tube going to uni. I felt scared as I walked though the familiar underground corridors and went down the same old stairs to the train. As I sat there, jerking side to side as the train moved to the next station, the mood around me was subdued and strained. I looked around at everyone in the carriage with me, worried that at any moment I could be blown up into 'pink mist' by some brainwashed psychopath and never see my parents again, but no one was looking around at each other; they were looking at ME.

What am I really? Just a small, fair skinned girl, who looks younger than she really is. What made me threatening? Was it my bag, bulging from all my books, folders and other crap? Was it my dark features? Or my prominent, long nose that identified me as being Asian? NO, it was the triangle shaped cloth that was wrapped around my head, which put me in the same box as the terrorists who had blown up innocent people a few days previously, in the name of my religion.

Several days later, my parents told me to stop wearing the hijab, because my mum heard from a friend that a young Muslim girl, who wore a headscarf, was attacked near where I live. Something told me that it was just a rumour, but I did as I was told, because deep down inside I didn't feeling safe wearing it anymore and didn't like the attention I was getting.

I felt like a criminal, a non-person, as though I were disfigured in some way to incur such stares and blatant hard shoulder. It was as if people I *didn't even know* were *ignoring me* and yet making it clear that they *knew* I was there, by the subtleties of their actions.

After taking my headscarf off, everything went back to normal, with regard to how I was treated by the public. Was it because I looked like an unthreatening, innocent girl? Was it because I had fair skin and didn't look like a stereotypical Asian? Would it have mattered if I did? NO, things went back to normal, because I wasn't wearing a triangle shaped piece of cloth over my head, which blatantly identified me as being Muslim and therefore a potential terrorist.

People forget that a lot of innocent Muslims *also* died that day. Maybe the government ought to have stressed that to help minimise the Islamaphobia that exists today.

I would love to say that everything was fine after I took my headscarf off but it wasn't. The side effect was that people at uni kept asking me *why* I no longer wore it and providing them with an answer that didn't sound pathetic was hard. I felt stupid as I explained that my parents made me take it off because of something they heard.

All my friends who wore the hijab still wore theirs and although they didn't intend to, I could sense that they were disappointed and were being slightly judgmental. Some of my non-Muslim friends said I looked better without it, which made my blood boil, but I kept my mouth shut. All in all, I felt like I had given into something, taken the easy route and copped out on doing the right thing.

The news and newspapers at that time were covered in the headscarf debate. There were issues going on in France and Turkey, as well as people's response to Sheikh Dr Zaki Badawi's advice to women in Britain to stop wearing the hijab, because of an increase in hate attacks since July 7th; "*Dress is meant to protect from harm, not to invite it*", he was quoted as saying.

Most Muslims who I talked to about the subject were outraged and felt that women should not give in to thugs who target them because of their hijab identifying them as being Muslim. They felt that the removal of the headscarf takes away a women's identity as a Muslim and that they should not have to *conform* to look like everyone else in a country that is *meant* to be free and accepting when compared to its eastern neighbours.

With all this drama happening in the world around me, I actually researched on the internet what Islam said about women covering their hair, because I was worried that I was going to hell. Eventually, I concluded that I was attracting more attention by wearing the hijab than I was when I didn't and that although I felt safe before 7/7 when I wore it, I didn't after due to the new political climate.

I listened to what my parents told me to do for my own safety and the Quran itself doesn't *list* the *exact* body parts to cover and show, which in my view is because how you dress depends on which country and time you are in. Cultures change and part of being Muslim is to inseminate into the country you are in and abide by their laws, while practicing your religion in a way that will not put you in unnecessary danger. Obviously this doesn't mean a Muslim should dress half naked if everyone around them is. What it does mean to me is that you should dress in a way where you are safe from persecution, fit in and are ensuring your modesty by covering the parts of you that don't appear naturally, in a way that you feel is still abiding by your religion.

I think it's really sad that a symbol such as the hijab acts like a warning sign to non-Muslims and puts them on edge. Even I, being Muslim myself, feel scared and uncomfortable when I see women in *full* head to toe Muslim dress. The media has been so successful in creating a climate of fear that I'm scared of *my own people,* which is pathetic. I'm ashamed to say that I stare and am scared with everyone else, but this is only because I'm human. If the media can make *me* feel that way about my own kind, I understand how others can and feel that if the media has the power to do that, it is also within their ability to reverse the damage it has done.

I dedicate this to all the head scarves that lay forgotten in my chest of draws. I haven't given them to someone else because I'm waiting for the day when I will be comfortable wearing them again.

About the Author:

Iram Riza Syed (I.R. Syed) is a BIT and Business graduate and is in the process of editing her first sci-fi novel entitled *Blood, Sweat and Tears,* which is the first volume of the *Blood, Sweat and Tears'* series. She lives and works in London as an Administrator and the anthology is the first published piece of work she has produced.

A Psychological Barrier?

©Jan Andersen 2008

Having lived all my life in Northern Europe and of no particular religious denomination, I have never had to conform to a strict dress code dictated by cultural beliefs or by the guidelines interpreted from a Holy book. The only time when I have had to wear a specific uniform was when I was at school and on the few occasions when I have attended a formal event that required a certain dress code. I have never read the Quran, nor was I previously familiar with the reasons behind the Islamic female dress rules, but had always assumed that it was to prevent men from looking at women in a sexual manner. One might ask, therefore, how I can be qualified to pass judgement on the hijab, jilbab, niqab or burka. However, in order to add some balance to this book, it is interesting to obtain the view of a non-Muslim and provide some insight into the way in which those of other faiths perceive the hijab, but even more particularly, the "veil".

As such, the hijab, when referring to the head covering, should never be an issue, since people of all cultures generally dress according to personal choice when it comes to dresses, trousers, shirts, scarves or hats. The main area of controversy with regard to Islamic dress appears to be the addition of the facial covering i.e. the niqab or the burka.

What I do believe in is freedom of choice, but what I don't believe in is individuals being condemned for those choices unless they adversely impact the lives of others. An example is the tragic case of female Pakistani minister, Zilla Huma Usman, who in 2007 was shot dead by an Islamic extremist for refusing to wear the veil. The perpetrator claimed that he was following Allah's commandment to kill all women who sinned, interpreting her failure to wear the veil as a "sin". (TimesOnline 1.)

Another example is Mahmoud Ahmadinejad's ascension to Iran's presidency in 2006, which heralded a crackdown on women who did not adhere to the strict Islamic dress code. Reports state that teams of patrols on the streets of Tehran and other large cities would confront inappropriately-dressed women and sometimes strike them with police batons before taking them into detention. Tehran's chief of police, Morteza Talaee, officially announced that officers would deal harshly with offenders of "the Islamic dressing values" and that even taxi drivers who transported "improperly clad" women would be punished. However, following this announcement, President Mahmoud Ahmadinejad released a statement supporting women's right to wear clothing of their choosing, saying, "We have a wise population of women in the Islamic Republic who are familiar with the values. There is no need to put any kind of pressure on them." (Boghrati 2.)

Then there was the case of a 24-year-old Muslim teacher, Aishah Azmi, who was suspended from her post at a Church of England junior school in Yorkshire in 2006 for refusing to remove her veil whilst teaching children. A council spokesperson claimed that both the teachers and children were finding it hard to understand what the teacher concerned was saying because of the veil. (Knight 3.)

In another case, a 12-year-old schoolgirl lost her attempted legal challenge against her Buckinghamshire school's ban on wearing the veil. Again, the teachers believed that it would make communication difficult. (BBC 4.)

In the previous two situations, I do believe that if the veil impedes a woman's ability to communicate effectively in a role such as teaching, where effective communication it is essential, then it should be removed. However, if she wishes to exercise her right not to do this, then perhaps she ought to consider a different profession in order to avoid conflict with authority.

There are some government laws that dictate what one should or should not wear. In Turkey, for example, where 99% of the population are Muslims, a ban on wearing hijab in universities and schools has been in place for a few years.

I have heard many people say that in a nation such as Great Britain where Islam is not the main religion, but has become more prevalent as a result of immigration, that people who refuse to abide by the cultural rules of this country should return to their own land. The feeling amongst some is that if a foreigner wishes to integrate into British society and avoid isolation, they should conform to the rules practised here. If a British woman attempted to exercise her right to dress as she pleased in a country such as Iran, for example, that would never be tolerated, so the thinking behind the above view is, why should it be tolerated in Britain?

Other people to whom I have spoken believe that wearing the veil is a brash or proud statement of identity, rather than a genuine religious observance, although I do not necessarily believe this to be true in the majority of cases.

One disadvantage, of course, is the more sinister motive behind someone people's choice to wear "shades" or head coverings. "Hoodies" have received adverse criticism recently because of their association with young criminals attempting to conceal their identity when committing offences.

I believe, therefore, that the burka has received a bad press in the West because of the assumption that the person behind the veil does not want her identity known for more sinister reasons than simply conforming to religious beliefs. We judge people by their faces and their expressions and I must admit that there is something slightly unnerving about talking to someone whose face is hidden. From a Westerner's perspective, it reminds me of villains in balaclavas, or with stockings over their heads. I am very much a visual person and love seeing people's faces and, of course, being able to gauge their reaction to what I am saying. It is very difficult to monitor someone's true feelings when you cannot see their face. People can hide so much with words, but their expressions generally convey the authenticity of what they are saying. When you can see someone's face, you are often able to assess whether or not they appear approachable and how they are feeling emotionally.

In support of the veil, there is something about covering part of one's face that elicits a feeling of greater security and confidence within oneself. I always feel more confident when wearing sunglasses or a hat. Is it because one appears more vulnerable when one's entire face or head is exposed? When you are wearing sunglasses, you can see whether people are staring at you without appearing as though you are staring back and, of course, you can weigh up other people without their knowledge. It's always difficult to determine exactly where someone is looking when they are wearing sunglasses, because you can move your eyes without having to move your head! You can also have a degree of anonymity. Until you see someone's eyes, you can never be entirely sure that they are not someone else who looks similar. Sunglasses can hide embarrassment and a range of other emotions that one sometimes wishes to keep secret. Similarly, a peaked or brimmed hat can be pulled down to shield one's eyes and, if your hair is your trademark, that too can be hidden.

I personally don't view the hijab as being any different to the headscarves worn by both young and old women in different ways, either tied beneath the chin or at the nape of the neck. Nor are they any different to other head coverings worn by members of different religions of both sexes, such as a Sikh's turban, a Catholic nun's coif, a Jew's yarmulke or a Hutterite's head scarf. Rather than protecting one's modesty, however, I have heard many men of different nationalities say that are attracted by the mystery of women who have their heads and faces concealed.

I believe that the world would be a far better place if we all respected each other's differing beliefs - dress or otherwise - as long as they are honourable and cause no harm to anyone. We might not agree with the principles of different religions and cultures, but that does not mean that we should not accept those who think differently to ourselves.

I do believe that you can have faith without following an organised, "controlling" religion, yet I have no problem with those who choose to follow a particular religion. After all, all souls are the same, irrespective of race, creed or the religion practiced. Most people would agree that the basis of all religion should be love, compassion, understanding and selflessness and if we all abide by those basic rules, then we should all be able to live alongside each other in harmony. I think it's terribly sad that a person's intentions should be judged by a piece of cloth on their head. We should, therefore, judge others by their actions, not by the clothes they choose to wear.

Works cited:

1. Female Pakistani minister shot dead for 'breaking Islamic dress code:' Times Online. February 2007.
    http://www.timesonline.co.uk/tol/news/world/asia/article1414137.ece.
2. Boghrati, Niusha. Islamic Dress Code to be Strictly Enforced.
    Worldpress.org. 2 May 2006. http://www.worldpress.org/Mideast/2334.cfm
3. Knight, India. Muslims are the New Jews. Times Online. 15 October 2006.
    http://www.timesonline.co.uk/tol/comment/columnists/india_knight/article 600860.ece
4. Schoolgirl loses veil legal case. BBC online. 21 February 2007.
    http://news.bbc.co.uk/1/hi/education/6382247.stm

About the author:

Jan Andersen is a Freelance Writer, Author and Editor specialising in commercial copy, website content, book editing and articles on diverse lifestyle topics and social issues. She has also participated in many TV and radio programmes. Jan also owns and runs numerous websites, including Mothers Over 40 (www.mothersover40.com)

She is the author of two fertility books and is currently completing a third book on the topic of child suicide. Jan has had four children and has three grandchildren. Her eldest son, Kristian, tragically took his own life on 1 November 2002. Her other children are a daughter aged 22, a son aged 21 and a daughter aged 9.

Uniform

© Sarah Butler

You know what it's like, middle of the night, the weight of the morning keeping sleep out of reach. You know what it's like, when time stretches a tight bubble around you – tangled duvet, cold toes – and refuses to move on.

I am sixteen-years-old. I can buy a lottery ticket, work full time and have sex. I am mature for my age; the teachers who say that are the same ones who look down their noses at mum, every parents' evening.

I lie and listen to the night buses. Our flat is on the fourth floor, but you can still hear the hiss of their doors and the heave of their engines. Mum says the walls are paper thin. She talks about double glazing like it's an exotic holiday destination.

Tomorrow I have to go to college. Not strictly true; I can leave school and get a job, but tomorrow I am going to a college, which until now has been a name on a form, a glossed prospectus and a half hour visit of white corridors, noisy drama studios and swinging double doors.

My room faces the street. At night, the light steals, dirty yellow, around the edges of my curtains and turns the contents of my room into shades of grey. The clothes on the back of my chair are charcoal dark shapes. It's hard to make them out, to separate one thing from the other. I didn't want to take the labels off, just in case, but mum got the orange kitchen scissors out and cut through every one of those thin plastic things. There's a pile of price tags in the bin by the chair. Mum spent more than she could afford.

I wake my phone up. It's 4:03am. I press my eyes shut and take deep breaths; one, two, three. I'll have bags under my eyes. I won't be able to concentrate. No one will want to talk to me.

33

Mum was trying to help, I know that. She watched me take my clothes out of the washing machine, shake them out and hold them up, trying to decide. It's about saying who you are, she said. It's about sitting there, on the bus, in your class and saying, "This is me."

My mum wears tops that show the deep line of her cleavage and the curve of her stomach. She wears jeans and wide belts; silver, red, orange. She has her hair done every month by a woman who lives on the top floor. The woman comes here to do it and when I get back from school the air smells chemical sweet and mum's happy because the blonde sections of her hair reach right up to the roots. I think she's prettiest when she takes her make-up off. She laughs when I tell her that. "I couldn't go out without my face on," she says and I think, "Imagine, if you had a face you took off at night and put in a box, ready for morning."

Who will they think I am? When I walk into a room called 'blue four,' which is where I have to be at 9 o'clock tomorrow morning, which is actually this morning, though it seems so far away. Who will they think I am? You think I'm over-reacting. You're wondering how come I've not thought about this before? Where have I been hiding the last sixteen years? I've been wearing school uniform, that's what. I do what I'm supposed to do; wear my tie this way or that way, loop silver rings through my ears, but that's copying, that's easy. Weekends? Holidays? I've never cared much and my friends aren't the type of people who bother about those things either. Jeans, t-shirts, nothing that would draw attention.

Mum's always tried to get me interested in clothes. She used to dress me up like some kind of doll when I was little, got my ears pierced with tiny gold studs, even put make-up on me sometimes. I used to squirm away from her hot fingers, scratch at lace against my neck, rub colour off my eyelids and pull at my knee high socks with the pink ribbons until the elastic snapped and they sank around my ankles.

Mum's got a double wardrobe in her room and it's crammed full of clothes. Next to the wardrobe, there's a table with a mirror above it; a mess of foundation, eye shadow, jewellery, perfume and lipsticks. She's always trying to take me shopping with her, but I can't think of anything worse than following her round TK Maxx and watching her pull out tight, bright stuff and declaring it was made for me. I love my mum, but sometimes she's too loud.

I don't know why I asked her to come shopping with me. This was yesterday. I couldn't stop thinking about college and how I wouldn't know anyone, and worrying about people looking at me and deciding I wasn't the sort of person they wanted to be friends with. I was distracted, a bit stressed out. If I'd thought about it I'd have known it would be a disaster. Anyway, I asked her. You should have seen her face. Not just her face; her whole body lifted, like she was lighter or something and for some reason it made me feel guilty.

4:20am. I'm taking English, History, Psychology and Sociology. Mum wanted me to do science or maths or business studies. Something useful, she said. But she's got French A level and works in Somerfield, so I figured I might as well do something I enjoy.

We got the bus to Oxford Street. She talked the whole way there; planning. I'd need a whole load of stuff, she said. She was so glad I'd asked her advice, which I hadn't. We might as well get rid of pretty much everything I owned; my blue sweatshirt that feels like a hug, my black jeans with tired knees. She'd pay for it all. I wasn't to worry about that. I let her talk.

This is the problem with my mum. On the one hand she says I have to think about what I'm going to wear because people will judge me on it; that what I wear is my statement to the world about who I am. On the other hand she's more than happy to take over and choose for me.

I won't bore you with the details, but it was painful. We went from over-heated changing room to over-heated changing room. Mum made me stand in the corridors so she could see. Eyes peeked from behind curtains. Shop assistants smirked. An ever growing collection of plastic bags bashed against my legs. Skinny jeans, cheap boots and a rainbow of tank tops, patterned shirts and zip up hoodies.

On my chair, in the ashy light of my room, lie black leggings, a black skirt - short and flounced, a yellow t-shirt made of that ribbed kind of material and a thin black wrap around. A pair of black and yellow pumps are on the floor, but you can't see them from my bed. Is that me? A wasp, irritating and stinging for no reason. Or perhaps a bee; they're useful at least, work as a team. I pull the duvet up around my chin and curl my legs in tight. I told you the shopping trip was awful, but afterwards, back home, choosing those clothes draped over my chair, that was different.

Usually I don't let mum into my room. It's a small room; it's a small flat. There's a single bed, a wardrobe with a wooden frame and a piece of material for the door, a thin desk by the window and a green plastic chair. All those bags of clothes nearly filled up what's left of the floor. We both went in without really discussing it. Mum sat on my bed and looked a bit awkward first of all.

"Let's have a look at them then," she said. "Let's pick out an outfit for tomorrow."

Have you ever had that thing when you're tired and worried and you're with the person you usually take that stuff out on and then you end up having fun? You end up smiling a bit, and then laughing, and you can say stuff that you'd usually keep locked inside your mouth because it might sound stupid. It was something like that. Mum chose

36

music from my iPod and held her fist up to her mouth
pretending it was a microphone.

"And she looks stunning! A summery number, casual
yet stylish; see how that blue brings out the colour of her
eyes. The boys are going to swoon."

For once she didn't annoy me. For once I played along,
pulled this top off, put another top on, pushed my legs into
tight jeans, flounced skirts and three-quarter length
combats. I turned on the spot. I pretended I was on the
catwalk. I pretended I could be anybody I wanted to be. We
chose the clothes that are now draped over the back of my
chair. It was fun.

The alarm on my phone snatches me awake into a
confusion of tinny dance beats. It's tomorrow. Today. If I'd
got a job in Somerfield, at least I'd have a uniform;
turquoise shirt, dark trousers and a badge with my name on.
I turn my phone off and lie, staring at the ceiling, very still.
I could pretend I'm ill. It's not too far off the truth, but then
I'd have to turn up tomorrow, or the day after and people
would look at me harder; of course they would. I'd have to
find a space to fit and the gaps would be smaller than they
will be today.

I turn the shower up too hot. Sometimes that makes me
feel better. Not today.

7:30am. Dressed. What do you think? The skirt's too
short? I'm trying too hard? My legs look fat? I look like the
kind of person you might want to talk to? You can be
honest. I want to know.

The only mirror in my room is so small it only just fits
my face in. I move around, trying to catch a look at myself,
but all I get are mirror-shaped pieces of black and yellow.

Mum's not a morning person. When I'm getting ready
for school, she's always sitting at the kitchen table in her
dressing gown, scowling, with her coffee and a cigarette.
As long as I don't try and ask her anything, we usually
don't fight. This morning though, the kitchen smells of

toast and she's made a pot of tea, already poured milk into my favourite mug. Her smile comes easily.

"You look gorgeous," she says, opening her arms and grinning and suddenly I know I have to get changed.

"Do you want toast? Tea?" She bustles around me.

Outside, the sky is flat blue. The sun throws in slabs of light between the slats of the blinds.

"They'll think you're quite the fashion guru, won't they? They'll think..." I zone her out; it's something I've learnt to do.

You know what it's like, upsetting people; the way your stomach slams downwards, the way the heat flashes across your skin.

"It's not that I don't like them, mum. It's just, I feel more comfortable in this."

8:30am. I'm wearing the faded black jeans and an old red top with a swirl of black flowers along one sleeve. I've switched the pumps for my trainers. The walk to the bus stop goes underneath a line of chestnut trees. There will be leaves to kick.

She opens her mouth, ready to shout, ready to list how ungrateful I am, how selfish, how frustrating, but then she closes it again, tight so the words can't get out.

"I'm sorry, mum."

"Go." She indicates towards the door with her head. "You'll be late. Don't want to be late."

I almost run back to my room and put the leggings and the skirt and the yellow top and the black wrap-around and the black and yellow pumps back on. I almost ask mum if she'll lend me some make-up. But it's too late for that. She doesn't walk to the door with me like she usually does. She stands just inside the kitchen and watches me. As I shut the door I think I hear her say something, but I couldn't be sure.

On the street, the wind rushes against me, tugs at my hair and the collar of my jacket. Do you have a favourite season? Mine's autumn. The cold edge to the air. The way the sun slices long shadows from the smallest of things. The way the colours spread through the trees like they're blushing. The bus is jammed full of people in coats they've pulled out from wherever they left them all summer. There's a man with a ribbed green hat, a white headphone lead trailing underneath a khaki t-shirt. There's a woman with a black headscarf held in place with a silver hair grip the shape of a flower. There's a woman with bright red cheeks, a huge cream jumper, blond hair fizzing around her shoulders. There's a girl, her hair plaited into tight lines along her scalp, a fur-lined hood making a bowl behind her. No one looks at me. I curl my fingers around the pole and brace myself against the heave and roll of the bus.

The girl with the hood gets off at my stop, right outside the college. We both hesitate amongst the swill of people, and I catch her eye.

"You going there?" She moves her head in the direction of the college; low brick buildings, bright blue painted window frames.

I nod. She's wearing tight jeans and expensive looking boots with furred edges and tassled laces. She's got a black leather bag with big silver buckles. A sheen of blue eyeshadow sparkles as she blinks.

"I'm Melissa." She jabs a hand towards me; thin black fingers. No rings. "English, media studies, business studies, art."

"Sam." I take her hand, briefly, almost laugh at the formality of it. "I'm doing English too."

We walk together towards the college building, find seats next to each other in room 'blue four,' which is actually a lecture theatre and not blue at all. It is crammed full of people. I lean towards Melissa and say, "I had a fight with my mum this morning."

"She wanted you to wear a suit?" Melissa's got a breathy kind of a laugh.

39

"She didn't want me to wear this." I gesture downwards. "We went shopping yesterday, and..."

Melissa shifts in her seat so she's half facing me. Her eyes flick down to my feet, then back to my face. I feel the threat of a blush; tears hovering. I'm not sure if I'm still breathing.

"She's just worried about you, that's all," Melissa says. "My mum practically spat on her handkerchief and wiped my face before I left. And then it was, 'Melissa, your trousers too tight. Melissa what those boys going to think, your top so low like that?'" Her laugh tilts upwards and I draw air deep into my lungs.

A woman wearing a pale pink headscarf bangs on the table at the front of the room and the noise starts to die down. She is head of pastoral care at the college, she tells us; we are all very welcome and she hopes we will be happy here. She's a small woman, but her voice is loud and clear and her smile reaches all the way to her eyes. As I listen, I imagine a drawer full of scarves for her, every shade of every colour. I wonder if she decides which one she'll wear in the morning before she goes to sleep at night. I wonder if she worries about what people will think when they look at her. I wonder if she's got a daughter. I picture her; a shorter, thinner version of the woman at the front. Does the head of pastoral care try to tell her daughter what to wear? Does she take her shopping and embarrass her beneath hot lights, amongst mirrors? Does her daughter have a drawer full of scarves too? I imagine the woman, who is smiling at us, telling us we've got two precious years ahead, watching her daughter leave the house, her hair caught up in a ponytail, or cut short around her face.

When I get home tonight, I'll put on the headband mum picked out yesterday. It's patterned like leopard skin, tiny black marks on a silver background. I'll make mum a cup of tea and offer to cook dinner. Maybe I'll make a chilli; she loves my chilli, says it's the best there is this side of Mexico, not that she's ever been. I'll tell her about today, about Melissa, about the woman and her pale pink headscarf and smiling eyes, about whatever else is going to happen between now and then. I'll ask her about her day. I'll wear the headband and she'll notice it, even if she might not say anything. I'll stay up with her, watch some TV. That way she'll know I'm sorry. That way she'll know we're okay.

About the Author:

Sarah Butler writes novels and short fiction and has been published by Route, pulp.net and Litro. She lives in London and runs UrbanWords, a literature consultancy, which specialises in projects using creative writing as a way to explore and question our relationship to place. You can find out more at www.sarahbutler.org.uk and www.urbanwords.org.uk.

The Magnificent Cloak

©Shakti Maya

I lived at *la rue Monsieur* in Port-Louis, the capital of
Mauritius, a multi-cultural island in the middle of the
Indian Ocean. As such, I had many Muslim neighbours and
school friends. Four Muslim families, who were my
neighbours, constituted a fundamental part of my view of
the world. They were the *Jeewas*, the *Ganthis*, the *Dobas*
and the *Motours*.

As I had many Muslim neighbours and school friends,
as well as lived in a very religious country, I knew some of
the principles and facts of Islam. I was well acquainted with
Eid celebrations. At the Islamic New Year, my neighbours
including Shamima and Shenaz would bring offerings of
plates of sweet vermicelli to my family. I knew about
Bakreid, Eid El Ada, when a bull is sacrificed to Allah and
the meat then shared three ways: with the family members,
with the community and with the poorer Muslim families.

Although I understood the meaning and significance of
this sacrifice and traditional ritual, every year I nonetheless
felt very sad and sorry for the animals. I would hear them
moo the day before and used to wonder about their
thoughts. I once asked Shamima about this. Even though
she was only one year younger than I, she knew a lot about
Islam. She used to go to *Maktab,* the special religious
classes on Islam, so she was very knowledgeable about
such matters. In her wisdom, Shamima explained to me that
the specialist who came to slaughter the bull was an expert
in making such sacrifices, so the animals did not suffer at
all.

Although I had great respect for the said expert and
specialist, I nonetheless could not help but feel sad and
anxious for these animals. Of course, I realised that this
was also their destiny. My grandma had indeed explained

43

to me how destiny works. You can't do anything about it. It is all written at your time of birth. I wonder if it is a higher calling to be chosen to be sacrificed for God. I am sure that it must be. I hope that the chosen bull knows and feels this honour, and hence has no fear and does not suffer at all when being killed. Even though I could not help but feel anxious, I was sure that between Allah and the specialist, the animals were well taken care of.

Shamima's wise explanations, Shenaz's illuminating examples and indeed my school friend Soraya's vivid stories about her family helped me understand a lot about the fundamental principles of Islam. My close personal interaction with my various Muslim neighbours helped me learn a lot by sheer observation and participation in their lives. However, what was a mystery to me as a child and still remains an enigma to be as an adult, is the *hijab*; not just the one that leaves the face, feet and hands exposed, but the *burka*, the one that covers the face too and leaves only the eyes exposed or indeed veiled. Of all the Muslim families I knew in Mauritius, only the *Motours'* grown-up ladies followed this tradition. So the combined knowledge of Shamima, Shenaz and Soraya was of little help to me.

The two *Motours'* girls, Mina and Farhzia, went to the same primary school as I did. They were, however, a few years older than I. Although we did not play with the same age groups of children at school, we used to exchange greetings whenever we saw each other and even chatted a little. A couple of times, I had gone inside the courtyard of their house at the end of my road. However, I have never seen any of the grown-ups there. Local gossip speculated that *Mr Motours* had three wives. I don't know for sure if this was true. Of course, I was far too prim and proper to ask either Mina or Farhzia about this.

I was about 6-years-old and going to the shop next to the *Motours'* house when it happened for the first time. Here a few inches away from me, the big solid grey aluminium gate suddenly opened slightly. Out came three gown clad ladies in close succession. They were dressed from head to toe in black. I have never seen anything like this before. I had never seen anyone wearing this kind of outfit before. Their gowns covered them entirely. Hastily, they moved from behind the tall solid door into the back of the mini van parked directly in front of the gate next to the pavement. The last figure seemed smaller than the previous two, but other than that, they were non-distinct from each other.

As the smaller figure was stepping up into the mini van, she turned her head slightly towards me. All I could see was a set of eyes surrounded by black cloth. I only caught a glimpse of her eyes, yet, to me they seemed the most beautiful eyes I had ever seen. I think that they were lined with black kohl, but as it all happened so quickly and as she also had a veil in front of her face, I could not be sure. However, even though I could not see behind her black *burka*, I felt her smile. I am not sure how I knew this. I just did. I felt her smile at me.

I stood transfixed on my spot on the pavement. But, I could feel myself beaming at the ladies. I am not sure how long I stood still on the pavement. Come to think of it, it could not have been more than a few seconds.

Shortly afterwards, Mina came out from behind the solid grey metal door followed by Farhzia. Both were not in normal dresses today, but in the traditional *shalwar kamiz:* long dresses with matching loose trousers and a scarf around their necks.

"Coumaniere?" said the always graceful Mina in *creole*, our native language, while the ever shy Farhzia only smiled at me.

"Mo korek," I replied, assuring them that I was indeed fine.

"Zotte pe alle promener?" I asked politely, enquiring about their intentions.

"*Nou pe alle ranne visite,*" winked Mina, letting me know that they were going out to visit relatives.

A few seconds later the mini van drove off.

Notwithstanding, more than thirty years later, the feeling of mystery still lingers in my heart.

The *hijab* still represents something so chaste to me. As a child, it conveyed to me a deep sense of sheer mystery. But three decades on, as an adult, rather than mystery, the *hijab* represents protection and purity. This may not have much or indeed have anything to with their real significance, but this is simply how I feel today.

As a teenager and in my twenties, I had often heard the *hijab* to be associated with the oppression of women by men, with the hindrance of the rights and value of women by political regimes, or indeed even by religious communities. Although I understand and perhaps can even agree with some of these arguments, to me the *hijab* represents something else. Even though, I have so far only met a few very interesting ladies from Malaysia, who shared with me their personal choice to wear the *hijab* when they were adults, I have not yet had the opportunity to speak with anyone who wears the *burka*. I would indeed love to do so; to hear their voices. I sometimes wish that as a little girl, I had had the audacity to enquire more about the ladies in Mina and Fahzia's family. All I knew then was that as my friends were not yet married, they did not have to wear the *burka*. I assumed that as one day when I grew up and got married, I would wear the *saree*, they would in turn wear the *burka* when they got married. It was all rather straightforward.

In my current ignorance of its religious meaning, the *hijab* represents the protection of purity to me.

A few years ago, during a particularly challenging phase of my life when I felt very vulnerable, I longed for the religious privilege of wearing the *burka*. I wanted to put a barrier between the outside world and me. I needed an added layer of protection. I craved for an added shroud of emotional as well as physical safety. Unfortunately, as I was not a Muslim, so I did not feel then that this option was available to me. Still, thinking about it now, about seven years later and from the standpoint of being a much stronger and wiser woman, I know that had I walked past a shop selling *burkas* then, I would have probably, without meaning any disrespect, bought one for myself there and then.

A word that I personally associate with the *hijab*, in particular the *burka*, is purity. To me, the *hijab* enables a woman to remain untarnished physically by the outside world. I wonder if I am completely deluded! Still, the *burka* conveys to me an air of chastity. Of course, I know that married women also wear *hijabs* and *burkas*. But to me, regardless of the latter reality, there is an air of purity, which this garment simply conveys. Perhaps metaphorically, the *hijab* reminds me of the uniform gown, which the chaste nuns of the Christian faith wear. I wonder…

I have often thought about the differences with which people behave towards one another. I wonder if and how differently people react to the ladies wearing the *hijab* or the *burka*. Do people stop to think about the person behind the black cloth? What are the interactions like? Are they different to the ones that people have with me with my flowing long black hair and feminine skirts? Do people tend to be more respectful, as I find myself being, with people who wear the *hijab*? Alternatively, do people in fact fail to feel that a person is present behind the black cloth of the *burka*? Are people rude or abrupt to those whom they cannot see physically? Are interactions more personal or easier when you can actually see the face of the person wearing the *hijab*, as opposed to those whose faces are hidden behind the burka's veil? So many questions float in my mind.

I know very little about the religious and cultural significance of the *hijab*. I have heard many perspectives. Some, I have listened to intently. Others, I have dismissed promptly. Still others, I have ignored. Notwithstanding, I know how I feel. And to me, although the mesmerised 6-year-old girl I was has grown up, the *hijab* and in particular the *burka* still remains a mystery.

Perhaps one day I shall find out for myself whether the *hijab* indeed grants protection and purity. Perhaps I shall get the opportunity to speak more to the women who wear it: those upon whom the *hijab* has been thrust because of their birth and family tradition; those upon whom the *hijab* has been thrust because of political and cultural changes, but even more heartily, I would be blessed to speak with those who have chosen to embrace the *hijab*.

Until then though, the *hijab* remains a mystical and magnificent cloak to me.

About the Author:

Shakti Maya was born in Mauritius and lived there until at the age of 19, when she left in search of home. Over the years, her search has taken from Southern Africa, to Europe, to South America, then back to Europe. She has been living in the UK since 1995. Her journey is currently in transit in London. She has been writing for many years about the issues concerning women.

Her earliest memory of the *hijab* is when she was a child growing up in Mauritius. In fact, she was about 6-years-old when she first saw a *burka*. As a child and then woman, she has been both perplexed and mesmerised by the *hijab*.

Young Voices from Central Foundation Girls' School

From 2006-2008, I was Writer in Residence at Central Foundation Girls' School in Tower Hamlets. As part of the residency I worked with Anne McNulty, the Literacy Development Co-ordinator, on a project called Exploring the Unthinkable. Anne and I had a vision to take the Diversity and Equalities' Policy off paper and into practice, to embed into the school curriculum, to enable the issues of Diversity and Equality to be explored through the subjects of Political Literacy, Drama, Art and Music.

As a result, there were several pieces of writings that students wrote, accompanying artwork that reflected the issue of the veil/Hijab, expressed in different ways according to each individual's perception of what it means to them. It is always rewarding for me to find young people interested in writing to express the issues that they feel are of great concern to them. Their interest in writing is a step towards forming their own sense of self esteem and literary empowerment.

Rabina Khan

Princesses

My piece of work is based on my own experiences. Don't judge someone on how they look, but on what their personality is like. I chose this subject because girls face big problems because of the way they look and dress. It doesn't matter if you're fat or thin. We should just be happy with what you look like and how you are. This also applies to a person's race and religion and other forms of discrimination. Nelson Mandela fought in South Africa against the apartheid system so that all people could love equally side by side. I believe all people have a right to live in a non-judgmental society.

Dhiba Begum

It's Your Choice

My piece of art work is about not to judge people by just looking at them and it does not matter what kinds of clothes you wear. Many Muslim women choose to wear different clothes. Some choose to wear the hijab and others prefer western clothes. We should allow each other freedom of expression. My question is about how you choose what to wear.

Shahanara Begum 8T

Stereotypes of Muslim Women

In my art piece I have 3 different women from different religions, all wearing a veil in a way that suits them. They all look different yet beautiful in their own way. With this artwork I am trying to send a message to all those people who have prejudices held against Muslim women in veils. I am also trying to challenge people's perceptions of each other. Ask yourselves the following questions:

Why do you think Muslim women wear veils?
Do you think they are forced?
Do you have perceptions that need to be challenged?

For me personally the veil or scarf is like a friend. I choose to wear it of my own free will. Wearing the veil is

51

like having a special honour in itself. It is a part of my life which I cannot forget!

This project has taught me and made me realise how much I admire my religion and the veil. It has also taught me how to challenge people with prejudices against the veil.

Shuchita Ahmed 8T

Woman in Islam

My piece of work that I made is headscarf and it's about my religion Islam. I designed it with images, text writing and pictures to show to other people that I want to teach what it is like to be Muslim. It shows a lot of things that I do, to show you what you should do as well and the message is called 'Women in Islam'.

Thania Mirza 9I

Come Together

In my piece of artwork, it has a large number of countries with no borders on a dress, to show that all countries are equal. No one country is better than the other. That's why I took the borders away from the countries. All the countries should come together and re-unite as one. I added colour as well to still make it stylish and to show the importance of world equality. COME TOGETHER!

Mukshina Ahmed 9L

Women are the Foundation for the Structure of Life

I made a dress using clay to build it up. It is covered in pictures and writing explaining what all women want, such as respect, rights, love, equality and basically a life that they can run. All around the world not all women have equality because they are found powerless and vulnerable, but some are lucky to have been loved. For example, women are expected to love and have no love given in return because they are women. They are expected to be invisible for the world and visible to their own family in Islam and I think that is just committing you to prison for life. So I believe women can fight for everything they want.

Sidratul Alom 9I

Hoodies & Goodies

I have created my artwork because I feel that teenagers are discriminated against because of the way they dress. Older people see teenagers as troublemakers and nuisances. Everyone has the right to wear what they want so why do people stereotype all teenagers just because some individuals misbehave? We need to have a more positive attitude towards teenagers and give them the chance that they deserve.

Anika Tahsin 9L

Passionate

I am making a skirt because I want people to understand how women should be able to make their own choices about fashion and not feel under pressure from men or each other. It can only happen sometimes in certain cultures e.g. Asian countries. Women should be able to be allowed to express their own identity. To quote Annie Lennox: "Sisters are doing it for themselves."

Moshrat Jahan 9L

Equality

My artwork is a man's and woman's T-Shirt. One half is a man's and the other half is a woman's. This is to represent equal rights for both men and women. Some people believe that women have fewer rights than men. For example, there are not as many women in parliament as there are men. Also there are some women in Afghanistan that are controlled by men under the Taliban, but I want to show that they are equal.

Marjana Uddin

My Vision is Being Blurred

When I slept I dreamt.... I saw...
A woman
Strolling down the street emerging with the night sky,
With only an owl's eye to stare at the mouse.
Looking down and glaring into its miniature eyes,
It's anxious and afraid.
A lonely creature glides with the wind to a position where
It'll creep down, with a tip toe,
A step closer
Down to its nose.
Spread the wings gifted by the unseen so wide,
Swipe it so close to its mouth and
BITE!
On its tail.
Take a little creature to a land where only high trees and
dark caves exist,
With friendless creatures up above
And cowardly beasts in dark corners,
Where the owl is known to the mouse as friendless,
Where the lions are roaring throughout the day and night.
The mouse sees the lion crashing the gentle wings of an
owl,
Until the earth shakes and finally the trees come
Tumbling down.
Finally, the lions grip and savage through the owl.
One whisper is all that it took for me,
"Allah is the almighty."
I awake... with one gentle
Tap.
When I slept,
My vision was blinded, bat like.
When awoke from my dreaming world,
I did not see the owl emerging with the night sky,
But standing bright with the moon

With its beauty hidden behind the twinkling stars.
The lions were not roaring, but uttering the words of the almighty.
The beauty of an angelic wing was not crushed by the lion.
He lowered his gaze,
Allowing the one in a million,
Allowing his left rib to fly back
High into their tower where they can see the beauty of which a lion can only dream.
Their love of the stars, sky and the air protects them from a beastly animal.
A man.

©Hamida Yasmin
11U
Central Foundation Girls' School

The Hijab and Feminists

©Penny Wrout

I am a British baby-boomer - born in 1961 into a society that was finally busting out of the economic and social constraints that had dominated previous conformist generations. My sister and I were born into a farming family and while our parents probably hankered for a son to take on the farming mantle, they never let us know that.

We grew up with the expectation that we would learn whatever was necessary to help around the farm. Science, engineering and woodwork were options if we were interested. The unspoken hope may have been that one of us would someday take the plunge and follow the family tradition into farming, though in truth the only pressure was to work hard at whatever we did. By the time my brother came along, I was nearly 13 and the die was cast. We two older children had been brought up as proto-feminists; we saw no reason to doubt that women were capable of anything men did and we expected equal treatment.

Feminists and hijabs don't mix easily; at least they didn't in the 1980's. I was definitely among those women who saw that women were bold and strong, the equals of men in all intellectual and most physical fields. Yet I embraced the notion that women who chose to cover themselves for religious reasons were either physically oppressed or brainwashed by male-dominated institutions. I saw no contradiction in those views.

Then, in the mid-80's, I spent a summer working on the Palestinian West Bank. I was teaching English to teenage girls, most of whom wore traditional clothes of one sort or another and many covered their heads. I'd expected attentive learners, grateful for a little extra help. What I got were energetic, enthusiastic and sometimes very loud schoolgirls, falling over themselves to find out anything they could about the world beyond their tightly-constrained boundaries, and happy to pick up as much English as they could en-route.

The zest for life these teenagers manifested at the drop of a hat, matched my own youthful energy. Our hopes and dreams weren't dissimilar either - indeed their ambitions extended rather further than mine. Most wanted to be teachers or doctors, to serve their families, their community and God. I felt a little humbled before them, since they seemed to be granting their lives a higher purpose than I'd given mine.

This was the point at which I started to see through the veil; to recognise that underneath every scarf is an individual. And individuality embraces humanity and its full array of glorious, myriad difference. There are good and bad women who wear the hijab, just as there are clever and stupid ones, beautiful and ugly ones, oppressed and liberated ones.

But why is the hijab such a barrier to people from other cultures seeing that individuality? Perhaps it has something to do with how we read uniforms. In Britain, most people who wear a uniform expect to be identified primarily by those clothes when they put them on. While I'm wearing my policeman's tunic, my chef's hat, my nurse's apron, my football strip, I expect to be treated first and foremost as someone in that role. Without the relevant garb I'm just me. Maybe we struggle to get beyond the primary definition of 'Muslim' when we see a woman wearing Islamic clothes, and end up defining her solely through her religion?

One example that always amuses me is the amazement of the Western media, that sales of glamorous underwear are high in wealthy Muslim countries. As though Islamic women stop seeing themselves as attractive, or stop wanting to dress up, to indulge themselves, compare themselves or to please their husbands. Feelings and

58

desires may be expressed differently in different cultures, but let's not forget we all share fundamental human drives. But perhaps this tendency to brand women wearing any kind of veil as first, foremost and only Muslim, comes simply from a lack of familiarity. Inner Londoners pride themselves on their multiculturalism and inclusivity, yet many, particularly in the 40+ age bracket, have few real friends outside their own cultural boundaries. How many non-Muslims have visited the homes of practicing Muslims, eaten together regularly, worked closely with them or visited a mosque?

Forgive me if I sound smug, but my job has given me an advantage here. Over the years I've had chance to visit and work alongside a number of observant Muslim women. I've enjoyed the company of some and dreaded the time spent with others. So far, so normal, when it comes to work colleagues. And maybe it's that very normality that is the key. Since these collaborations are unexceptional, routine, everyday, I barely even notice the hijab, while I do recognise the strengths and weakness of the individual wearing it.

Yes, I know there will be observant women with whom I am never likely to share any degree of intimacy. We are separated by language, education or class and the veil becomes a physical manifestation of that division. So what do I think of them? Here that experience of the Palestinian teenagers stands me in good stead, as I draw on limited, relevant experience from elsewhere. I can only conclude that the women I see covered from head to foot in black, struggling with their shopping and children in Bethnal Green Road, will be as individual as snowflakes behind their hijabs – and I hope many more feminists have arrived at that conclusion.

About the Author:

Penny Wrout is a journalist, who for the last 6 years has been Communities Editor for BBC London. Her work is aimed at ensuring the many diverse groups living in the capital receive appropriate coverage, which also involves taking an active part in BBC outreach and media literacy activities. Her interest in community affairs dates back to her role as a Home Affairs Correspondent for the BBC at the time of the Stephen Lawrence Inquiry. She has won awards for her coverage of community concerns and diversity issues.

Penny lives in East London. Her husband is a designer and they have one daughter.

The Integration of the Hijab into Police Uniforms

©Shahida Rahman

The tension between the extremists within the contemporary religious community is more intense today than it has been in roughly seven centuries. While most individual Christians and Muslims do not agree with the rhetoric of the extremists within their own faiths, many are finding that the divide between the two groups might have an unintended effect on their own daily lives. Muslim women living in Western countries have, in recent years, found this to be the case when they begin wearing the hijab, the traditional head covering worn by devout women of the Islamic faith.

The controversy over the wearing of the hijab happens almost exclusively within a very specific context, that most often being a context involving an institution that requires its members to wear a uniform. Police forces in many cities in the West have had to deal with the question of the hijab, as more devout Muslim women are becoming qualified uniformed police officers. When these women choose to wear the hijab, the question of how this practice can be made to fit into the police force's standard issue uniforms comes into play.

Those who support a woman's right to wear a hijab with the uniform of her respective institution point out that the hijab is non-intrusive. It only covers the hair, not the face. (The veil that covers the face worn by some Muslim women is called the "niqab," and is distinct from the hijab.) The hijab can be made of any sort of fabric, of any colour or combination of colours one chooses. In this way, it can easily be integrated into the uniform of any institution, being made to perfectly match the existing uniform.

Muslim women who join the police force or other armed military or paramilitary groups might have other factors, besides the look of the headpiece, to consider when finding a hijab that can be integrated within the group's uniform. One of the biggest concerns is the safety of the officer. Several models of the hijab have been designed with these needs in mind. The feature most appreciated by many of the women who wear the hijab with their uniforms is the use of a strip of poppers to help the hijab in place. This design allows the hijab to come free if grabbed by an assailant. Unlike the pins used on many other models of hijab, these enclosures minimise the potential for harm to the officer if she is involved in a physical altercation. Adjustments such as this to the traditional design of the hijab demonstrate how adaptable the headpiece can be to the various needs of the women who choose to wear the hijab while they perform their duties.

Supporters of the integration of the hijab into the police force's uniform point to precedent. Several police, military and paramilitary forces, as well as schools and medical staff around the world have successfully included the hijab as an option for uniformed personnel. Similar allowance has likewise been made for other religious groups that require specific adornment for adherents. A notable example of such allowance is the concessions made for Sikhs in the British army and police force, where the turban is an accepted part of the uniform. In fact, turbans are even permissible headgear for motorcyclists on roads in the UK, instead of the helmets that are otherwise required. This sets a precedent that seems to favour the acceptability of the hijab or other garments required on the grounds of devotion to one's religion.

Those who oppose a woman's right to wear the hijab as part of her uniform see the issue quite differently. Many point out that the whole point of a uniform is to make one member of the group as indistinguishable from another as possible. The word "uniform," they point out, means "not changing in form or character, remaining the same in all cases at all times." The idea of allowing a member of the group to wear religious emblems that denote his or her adherence to a specific religious group goes against the very purpose of having a uniform in the first place. Many who oppose the donning of the hijab with a uniform take a consistent stand, not allowing for religious emblems of any kind to be worn with the uniform. This includes the displaying of a cross or a Star of David as much as it does the donning of a turban or hijab. Some opponents of the hijab, however, fail to take such a consistent stand, and it is this latter view that has most raised the ire not only of the Muslim world, but of many in the West who value tolerance and freedom of expression in a multiracial, multi-faith society.

Amongst those who specifically oppose the integration of the hijab into a police force's uniform, though they do not necessarily oppose the display of all religious emblems, the arguments are not always as simplistically intolerant as they may seem on the surface. For some opponents, the problem does not lie with the hijab, but with the lack of understanding within the community in which the hijab might be worn. In these communities, some fear, the hijab might mean something different to the uninformed than it does to the wearer of the hijab or members of her faith. The reason for the opposition, in this case, is an impetus to protect the officer and the police force as a whole from undue negative attention. The late Dr. Zaki Badawi, Principal and Founder of The Muslim College and chairman of the Council of Mosques and Imams, agreed that, in such a situation, the removal of the hijab might be the wisest course of action. The purpose of the hijab, he points out, is to protect a woman from unwanted attention that might result in her harm. If it, instead, invites the sort of attention that will result in any form of molestation of the woman, then it is ultimately counterproductive.

Not everyone agrees with Dr. Badawi. If the problem actually lies in an uninformed public, they argue, then the solution is to inform and educate. To require the minority group to conform, in this case, results in continuing ignorance within the public. Many believe that the presence of women wearing the hijab or other traditional ethnic or religious dress in positions of responsibility within the community will do much to combat the sort of ignorance that leads to intolerance, and perhaps even violent acting out of those intolerant attitudes.

In France, the issue of the integration of the hijab into the uniforms of various institutions, most notably state sponsored schools, has served to strengthen the nation's commitment to secularism. The high profile cases in France have led to much discussion across the world about religion, culture and tolerance. To some, the move toward secularism is a positive step, preventing the primacy of any one religion over others. To other observers, secularism itself functions as a sort of state religion, equally stifling the expression of adherents to all more recognised religions. The French policy of excluding the display of all religious emblems by any uniform personnel certainly does not seem to speak of free religious expression, particularly when compared with the progress toward religious equality made in countries like Britain, where more open expression is being allowed to people of all faiths, even when donning a uniform.

This is not to say that Britain's police force is a perfect example of religious tolerance. In recent news, we have seen reports of complaints of bigotry based on both race and religion made against individual police officers, and even against the police force as a whole. Yasmin Rehman, the director of partnership and diversity for London's

Metropolitan Police, resigned her post in October 2008, saying that she had consistently been the victim of sex and race-discrimination.

In an even more disturbing development, the West Midlands Police Force faced charges of race-inspired harassment of a Muslim woman, Mrs. Mahfooz Bibi. Officers arrested Mrs. Bibi at least four times without cause. She finally filed a complaint when male senior officers insisted that she remove her hijab, even though this violated her religious commitments. The officers' lack of understanding about the hijab's significance was the subject of much discussion during the investigation into Mrs. Bibi's complaints.

Even so, great progress has been made within the police force in the UK. Twenty-three-year-old Rukshana Begum, a special constable in Cambridgeshire, has recently seen her choice to wear the hijab become a matter of public concern when it was featured prominently in the news. When she began wearing the hijab on duty, the general public responded very positively, even approaching her to wish her well. Rukshana's experience, she says, gave her more confidence and helped her to feel more solidarity with the community. Besides this progress for Rukshana and the police in Cambridge, the Metropolitan Police in London has made allowance across the board for the wearing of the hijab and of ankle-length gowns as part of the uniform for Muslim women. Additionally, Muslim on-duty officers are now allowed to pray, to demand halal food and to have altered meal schedules during Ramadan. Scotland Yard's official policy has allowed the wearing of the hijab as part of the uniform since 2001. All of this speaks to Britain's commitment to freedom of religious expression for adherents to all faiths, making her a more truly multiracial, multi-faith society.

Rukshana's case in Cambridgeshire is instructive to those who fear that police officers who wear the hijab will face undue negative attention. Her request to wear the hijab was often highlighted in the media up until the day she began to wear the hijab as part of her uniform. When she was seen in public with the new addition to the uniform, many strangers approached her, not with negative comments, but with positive words of support and encouragement. According to Rukshana, this creates a feeling of solidarity with those she meets on the street, regardless of what their own religious affiliation may be. Her choice to stand by her own convictions has earned the respect of the community around her. Furthermore, by choosing to wear the hijab, and by having her case garner so much attention, she has actually helped combat the uninformed stance that might lead some to react negatively to seeing a hijab as part of a police uniform.

Muslim women living in the West have often been surprised by the misperceptions some of their neighbours have of the hijab. Asna Kadir, a nurse working in Norway's Stavenger University Hospital, wears a hijab to work as part of her uniform. The hospital has integrated the hijab as part of the uniform for all who choose to wear it. Kadir reports that when she began wearing the hijab, she did not receive any negative reaction, but many patients were curious and asked her questions about it. The most common question, she says, was whether or not she was forced to wear the hijab. She always answers this question with a firm "no."

The two most common misperceptions about the hijab, as reported by a number of Muslim women who have discussed it with curious Westerners, are that it is compulsory (perhaps even that women are made to wear the hijab by force), and that it is a sign of oppression. Both of these notions, however, have nothing to do with reality. The wearing of the hijab is strictly voluntary. There is some debate in the Muslim world about whether the hijab is required in the Quran, but most today agree that it is a woman's choice whether she will wear a hijab and when she will wear it. There are some, in fact, who wear the hijab in their private time, but not in the work environment. This is what Rukshana was doing before she requested permission to wear her hijab on duty.

The notion that the hijab is a sign of oppression is strongly denied by nearly all Muslims, both men and women. The hijab is, rather, a sign of a woman's devotion to her religion and her commitment to modest living. For many Muslim women, as Dr. Badawi has pointed out, wearing the hijab is a way to avoid attracting undue attention from men to whom they are not related. This is one expression of a Muslim woman's depth of devotion to her faith. And, as many Muslims like to point out, it is not very different from practices that have only relatively recently fallen out of favour in both Jewish and Christian communities.

A better understanding of the purpose of the hijab, and a woman's freedom to choose whether or not to wear it, will help change the perception of the Islamic faith and the women who adhere to it. Such understanding, it is hoped, will make it much easier to navigate through the controversies that will inevitably arise, such as those surrounding the integration of the hijab into the uniforms of police forces throughout the Western world, perhaps even helping Rukshana's experience of support from her community to become the norm. In the volatile times in which we live, finding peaceful solutions to such controversies can only be seen as a positive move. Perhaps proper handling of these controversies with mutual respect and understanding will even point the way for us to address the larger-scale controversies and prevent negative, polarised rhetoric from carrying the day.

Works Consulted

"Association of Muslim Police in the UK applauds Muslimah cop handshake refusal -Imam assures public she will touch man who is shot" *Militant Islam Monitor* website. January 26, 2007.
http://www.militantislammonitor.org/article/id/2682   Accessed on January 10, 2009.

Hijab in the News.
http://www.soicnanj.org/nj/index.php?option=com_content&view=category&layout=blog&id=34&Itemid=71   Accessed on January 10, 2009.

The Hijab Shop, articles.
http://www.thehijabshop.com/information/article1.php Accessed on January 10, 2009.

"Muslim Woman Police Officer Files Racism Charge in UK." *Thaindian News* website. October 19, 2008. http://www.thaindian.com/newsportal/world-news/muslim-woman-police-officer-files-racism-charge-in-uk_100108991.html Accessed on January 10, 2009.

National Association of Muslim Police. Press Release, November 13, 2008.
http://www.namp-uk.com/ Accessed on January 10, 2009.

"PC Rushkana Receives Warm Welcome from Cambridge Public." Islam Today website. July 17, 2007.
http://www.islamtoday.com/showme2.cfm?cat_id=38&sub_cat_id=1330 Accessed on January 10, 2009.

"Wearing the Hijab with the Police Uniform" *The Hijablog* website. September 27, 2008. http://thehijablog.wordpress.com/2008/09/27/wearing-the-hijab-with-the-police-uniform/ Accessed on January 10, 2009.

"West Midlands Police 'Racist' - Alleged Systematic Abuse" Indymedia UK website. May 18, 2005.
http://www.indymedia.org.uk/en/2005/05/311395.html Accessed on January 10, 2009.

"Women Hit Back Over Hijab Ruling." BBC News. August 4, 2005.
<http://news.bbc.co.uk/2/hi/uk_news/4742869.stm> Accessed on January 10, 2009.

"Women in Islam" *Islam for Today* website.
http://www.islamfortoday.com/women.htm Accessed on January 10, 2009.

About the Author:

Shahida Nessa Rahman was born in December 1971, in Cambridge, two days before East Pakistan became Bangladesh. She has three older brothers and a twin sister, who passed away at the age of 25. Her father arrived in the UK in 1957 and her mother in 1963.

Shahida has been writing since 2003 and self-published her first book in 2004 called, *Ibrahim – Where in the Spectrum Does He Belong,* published by Perfect Publishers. It tells the story of her eldest son who grew up with Semantic Pragmatic Language Disorder (SPLD), an autistic disorder. It highlights the lack of awareness of this condition within our society, but particularly within the Asian community where autism is not widely recognised. *Ibrahim* is included on the National Autistic Society's list of publications.

Her first historical novel, *The Lascar,* was one of four to be shortlisted, out of 10,000 entrants for the Muslim Writers Awards, 2008, Unpublished Novel Category. She has written a number of articles and most recent articles published are *Speech Disorders in Bilingual Children, The Lascars – The First Asians in England* and *Currying Favour.* She is also an associate of Silsila Productions Ltd.

Shahida still lives in Cambridge and is married with four children - three sons; Ibrahim, Imran and Aniq and a daughter, Aminah. She regularly helps reception children read at her children's school.

www.shahidarahman.co.uk

EPIPHANY/I'pifani/n

1996 – 2006 - Thoughts of a Decade

©Ruzina Ahad

Someone once told me,
"Look within yourself and believe that you are beautiful,
Then others will think you are beautiful too."
I have searched my soul,
I found nothing.
Is this what people think I am, a nothing?
"Follow your dreams" was another one
I've always believed in "following my dreams,"
But when people object to it,
It's hard to maintain that enthusiasm.
If I could have one wish,
It would be to have everlasting happiness,
But that won't make me human
Will it?
Everyone needs their happiness, every now and again
Otherwise there would be no sunshine after the rain.
No flashy word can help to express you,
Nor would your perfectly photogenic face
Reveal the true picture of you.
So my advice is….
Well, I don't have any;
Only you can make rules to abide by.
Meanwhile,
Cherish your thoughts and beliefs.
Cherish your perfect moments.
For there may never be another.
Live for tomorrow
For the past is only part of your future.
Don't try to prove yourself to others,

For you are proof enough.
Don't ever try to prove love;
You will never succeed.
Don't try to alter yourself,
You will only become confused.
Your minor faults could be seen as an attraction
To someone else's eyes.
Never lose your imagination,
Nor your ability to smile
And when you reminisce your past,
Remember with a smile,
For you will realise that living your life was
Worthwhile.
And, finally, live in gratitude,
For I like to think that we all live in a
Blessed world.

September 1999

I Believe

I believe that you should fight for what you believe in
Until the point where it seems that what you believe is
wrong.
Your battle then, is to challenge your injured values.
I believe that we should never be ashamed to admit when
we are wrong.
We are human,
Therefore, it is in our nature to err.
I believe that we should always look towards the greener
side of the field,
But only if it truly exists.
There is no point in living in fantasy,
For in the end, it is you who will be drowned in your
shattered dreams.
Somewhere, deep down, I do believe in true love,
But I believe that it is a rare luxury
And the reason why we say that 'love is blind'
Is because we never see things for what they really are.
Most of us just settle for a cheap imitation,
But then again, I believe that sometimes it is good to settle
down for second best,
But only if it is the second best thing in the world.
I believe that as much as you love someone,
That someone may never love you back.
That's why it's better to live without, than live with a
compromise,
Then, in due time, we will see that all this pain is actually a
blessing in disguise.
I believe in fate,
I believe that some things are beyond our capacities,
I believe that sometimes when bad things happen
They don't necessarily happen to us, but they happen for
us.
I believe that you should always go with your intuition

And you should accept certain things, for some things
should not be questioned.
I believe in Allah;
He is forever protecting me, guiding me and loving me.
I believe that even when I don't pray,
A prayer utters by itself.
I believe in death,
But I believe that our souls go on living forever;
Everything else just fades away,
Even memories....

August 2002

My Deceased Heart

They told me that I had decease in my heart, that I was
about to die,
So I reached out for Allah subhana wa tala, and to him I
began to cry,
But on failing to feel his warm presence,
I had to wonder why.

Was it because I had acknowledged my Lord's superiority,
But never gave Allah the opportunity to rule over me?
Was it because I read the Holy Quran and yet failed to act
accordingly?
Or never bothered to thank him when I ate out of his
bounties?

Was it because I never dressed or acted like a true Muslim?
Declared my love for our beloved prophet, and yet did not
make an effort to follow him?
Was it because I was too selfish with my wealth?
Was I too greedy, too miserly and never took time to think
of anyone else?
Did I lie, cheat and betray people's trust?
Did I backbite? Was I ever jealous of others and did I only
love out of lust?

Did I swear that the shaytaan was my enemy?
And yet when he offered me his temptations, did I even
resist?
If I really believed in Judgement Day, Jannah and
Jahannam,
Then why did all my actions in life reflect that they did not
even exist?

Was it because I claimed to love my creator, when in secret
I only loved his created?

Was it because I buried my own dead and never once learnt
a lesson from it?

Was it because I was so busy looking at other people's
flaws
That I forgot to see my own?
Lived like I would live forever, only to find out now that
this life is almost gone?

Maybe I could start all over again, begin tomorrow with
your glorious name?
I'm begging you, oh merciful, remove me from this pain.
I want to mend my broken heart, but they tell me that
there's no cure.
"Why is Allah ignoring me?" I ask. Is this heart of mine not
pure?

4 December 2003

Devil's Advocate

*"Whoever rejects evil and believes in Allah,
has grasped the most trustworthy handhold that will never
break"*
(Q2:256)

She was dancing with the devil
And she didn't even know it.
She claimed she was a believer,
But she didn't even show it.
While the one eyed beast played games with her,
The truth she once knew
Drifted away further and further.
Knowing that vanity was man's greatest sin,
She played the devil's advocate, because she thought she
could win.
Whilst the promise of the kingdom
Faded away like a distant dream,
She kindled with fire by calling out to the Jinns,
Deeper into the pit, unaware she kept falling.

Or so it seemed,

For last night she soured that sky
With angels wings.
Like a new born eagle she found
New meanings.
Like a phoenix from the ashes,
She rose from the dust.
She recited Quran and in Allah she put her trust.
She rectified her Iman
And vowed she will never be lost.
Silently she waged Jihad,
Her weapon and strength was embedded in her hijab.
She smiles at herself proudly,

Knowing she gave up worldly lusts.
Glorified be he who rose her from the dust,
Who gave her the courage to put her Deen first,
Removed her from his wrath so she may walk the straight
path.

As she looks at the mirror, she sees a woman removing her
mask,
But who will dance with me now?
The devil asks.

21 June 2006

She in the Mirror

Like butter wouldn't melt, she stands guilt free;
She admires her pretty face, but truly, who is she?
He veil she adorns, hides her sins,
She knows she's dirty, but she's immune to pretending.

She prostrates to her Lord, still guilt free,
Not thinking for a second that Allah is the almighty.
What happened to those days when your conscience was
clear?
You did what you did and repentance was rare.

A passing thought brushed away with her hair,
She in the mirror, she doesn't care.

16 October 2005

About the Author:

Ruzina Ahad is an emerging poet, artist and designer of Islamic women's clothing. She owns and directs *Just Jilbabz*, a fashion and Islamic clothing business based in London. Ruzina is the designer of various exceptional Islamic wedding garments and evening wear. Her poems are part of a wider collection of observations of a young Muslim woman living in modern Britain. These particular poems in relation to the Hijab/veil have been further developed to encompass a coming of age experience. The poems are just a reflection of the many facets of the poet who penned them.

Judge

©Ayesha Mazumder

Roses as beautiful as they are bare thorns,
Time as precious as it is moves on,
Doves as white as they are get dirty,
People as clever as they are make mistakes.

Everything has its downside,
But also has its upside,
Some upsides fool you,
Some downsides obscure your vision.

We judge so easily,
The more beautiful the better,
The uglier the worse,
Don't let looks fool you.

Looks can be deceiving as they say,
Look inside, what do you see,
A heart that is cold and black,
Or a heart that makes yours skip a beat?

Don't judge, it hurts,
Religious or pretty,
Fat or ugly,
Friendship first,
Looks last!

Who are we to judge?
The main judge is up there;
Judging takes place after death,
Not in this world!

Dead Veils

©Ayesha Mazumder

Why do you judge her by her veils
And not what kind of blood runs through her veins?
It's not about what she wears;
It's about who she fears.

Lying on the floor as cold as ice,
Never being allowed to use those eyes,
Blood running down her neck,
Not being allowed to move again.

Object lies on the floor,
 Two meters from the door,
A strong smell of petrol coming from the door,
Looking down at her body, burn on her neck.

Touch the cold handle of the door,
Step into the hall,
Spot a mirror on the corner of your eyes,
Running straight to it without a glance.

You are not the same girl,
You are a girl with veils,
A total stranger to your
          SELF!!

About the Author:

Name: Ayesha Mazumder
Age: 15
School: Central Foundation Girls' School

My passion for writing started with my passion for reading. I love to read anything and everything. I feel reading helps me escape from the current world, helps me explore worlds that only one can dream of, but I was not always such a book worm; there was a time I hated books. Now I look back, I regret not starting to read earlier, because I have learnt so much from reading and if I had only started earlier I would have gained a lot more knowledge. Writing is the same for me as well. When I write, I create new worlds, dream new things, imagine new people and create different situations. When I am writing, I am in control, not just of myself but of a world where I could do anything just by writing a few words on paper. A sentence to sum me up; an everyday East End girl who explores new worlds every day.

An 'Un-Hijabed' Woman

©Preetha Leela Chockalingam

There is an aura of cleanliness that is seemingly attached to the Hijab. It appears to speak of discipline, of formality, of a lack of laziness and of spirituality. While some of this may be true, women are women and Hijab or no Hijab, there will always be things that we have in common. I especially noted this at an all woman's birthday party once, when the women who normally wore the Hijab in the presence of men, rejoiced in the freedom and in the indomitable spirit of womanhood and sisterhood and got us all to get up and belly dance. The mood was happy, the food wholesome and the jokes on men free flowing. It must be added that as soon as the party was over, the women returned to wearing their scarves so they could get on the tube, hop into cars and drive off back into a world where headscarves for them, felt like a must.

In India where I grew up, you did not really see women wearing the Hijab. You occasionally saw Muslim women covered from head to toe in a black burka, or you saw Muslim women in blindingly bright colours; mint green, turquoise blue, shocking pink, orange and shades of red and gold that typically characterises the Eastern happy spirit. If there was one thing that all Indian women had in common, it was a love of colour and they wore these with spirit. Indian men, on the other hand, mostly wore common shades of white, blue and beige. Being colourful was seen as the female thing; the stamp of a woman's presence.

My first step into the world of Hijab friends and acquaintances was when I first arrived in the UK in 1991. I had several classmates at Uni who appeared to wear a tightly wrapped headscarf around their heads. Intrigued, I read up on it and discovered that although there were multiple definitions and notions of why women wore it, some things remained: it was primarily seen as something that commanded respect and enforced modesty and protected a woman from being seen as a sex object. Controversial as that might seem to some, I began to look upon the Hijab with renewed interest. I thought back to times when I had shakily as a learner driver tried to drive through streets in India, only to have my nerves shaken further by leering men egging me on to commit errors or park incorrectly. Would the Hijab have helped me in those circumstances? I also wondered if it were truly possible for men to look past sex when it came to women and I remembered a famous line in 'My Fair Lady' when Colonel Pickering asked Higgins, "Are you a man of honour where women are concerned" and Professor Higgins retorted, "Is there a man of honour where women are concerned?"

This question was interestingly answered for me. In my class, there were twins from the UAE who both wore the Hijab. One of them was very witty and outgoing, while the other was serene and pensive. They attracted as twins the normal amount of attention that any set of twins do with questions like, "Do you know each other's thoughts?" or "Did you dress up as each other as kids?" Mostly, they attracted the attention of a Turkish guy who gradually started attending class on time, smartening himself, sharpening his act and sitting close to the twins. At first, we thought he liked them both and we used to joke amongst ourselves saying, "I guess the Hijab is not doing its job," but then we realised that he liked the outgoing, cheerful one with the twinkling eyes. He told his friends that he was attracted to her smile and her eyes. It wasn't the Hijab and it wasn't that the Hijab wasn't doing its job. He had tremendous respect for her, but whether he could see her hair or not made little difference to him, as it was her eyes and smile that attracted him. The Hijab might have given her an air of respect, but it most definitely did not take away her attractiveness. On the contrary, it enhanced her other features. Like most youthful love stories, it didn't get further than a university romance, but it taught me an invaluable lesson about being a woman; it's not the scarf or sunglasses that you wear, but the way you are.

Gradually getting used to seeing the Hijab, I didn't give it much thought again until I was in the working world and teaching. I arrived late one morning, just twenty minutes before my afternoon class and sat down to a wilted salad that I had hurriedly packed in the vain hope that, come lunch time, I would find it attractive. I then observed out of the corner of my eye, a nun talking to a student. Having schooled at a convent school in India, I was used to nuns becoming teachers, but I found it startling that here, without a convent to attach to, was a nun teaching. A few minutes later, the nun entered the staffroom and someone said, "Lamis, there's a student for you." I was amazed to hear the nun utter a mild expletive. She turned towards me and I realised that the nun wasn't a nun, but a woman in an Abhaiya.

As I got to know Lamis (our love of good food, happily bonding us), I understood that she wore the Abhaiya some days and just the Hijab with long skirts and blouses on other days. It depended largely on her mood. This flexibility amazed me, but with Lamis, it was easy come, easy go. As long as she looked modest and her hair was covered, it didn't matter that she wasn't consistent with the Abhaiya. Ironically, whenever she felt particularly conscious of her weight, she wore it warmly like a secure blanket. Despite frequently interchanging between wearing the Hijab with colourful clothes or wearing the Abhaiya, she always wore the Hijab. It seemed synonymous with Lamis.

Lamis's life has changed massively since then. She has lost tons of weight, she has separated from her husband, she has her own flat and she dresses with a chic, but modest sense of fashion that elicits gasps of admiration, but the

Hijab still remains. It comes off when it's just us women. I have never questioned her about the Hijab. I understand it.

It's the same sense of security that I derive from wearing a dot or a line on my forehead. I vary it with colours the same way Lamis wears Hijabs that match her skirts. It makes me feel safe and announces that I am a Hindu woman in the same way that her Hijab announces that she is a Muslim. A common friend of ours once asked her if she would ever consider taking the Hijab off. Lamis firmly replied that she wouldn't because it made her feel secure. I feel much the same about the Bindi, the mark of being a Hindu. And if this mark on my forehead or the scarf on her head provide a sense of unity, belonging, community and culture, which conjures up images of sisterhood, of womanhood, of good wholesome cooking smells, of family, of friends, of both good and bad emotions, a sense of unity with the Divine, and a sense of protection, then all women have a secret Hijab.

About the Author:

Preetha Leela Chockalingam was conceived in London and born in India. Missing her family and tiring of her irritable, junior doctor husband, her mother Chitra left the safe haven of the hospital grounds to give birth to her in India. This instilled in her a sense of pride in being born on Indian soil and caused her a lifetime of queuing at embassies for visas.

Coming back to the UK at the age of three months, Preetha lived here until the age of five, before being carted off to India once again by a newly qualified proud Indian father, who started his own hospital.

School was a mixed bag for Preetha who was initially bullied for not fitting in. Later, she was applauded for the same, when classmates realised that she was more than willing to play class clown and shoulder the blame for causing chaos. She enjoyed English and bunking games and hated being picked up by an ambulance when her medical parents had to work overtime.

Overall, a sense of dual culture right from the start, constantly quarrelling parents, endless aunts, uncles and cousins, schooling in an Irish Catholic Convent in India and studying further in the UK, not to mention working as teacher in London, have provided much inspiration for writing. Preetha works as a lecturer at London Metropolitan University where she does everything possible to sneak in a read.

www.ingramcontent.com/pod-product-compliance
Lightning Source LLC
Chambersburg PA
CBHW062011040426
42447CB00010B/2002

* 9 780095 572671 2 *